Homemade Baby Food

17 Wholesome Baby Food Recipes for Easy, Nutritious, and Delicious Homemade Baby Food

by Janie Gleeson

Table of Contents

Introduction

The introduction of solid foods to babies is one of the most important milestones in a baby's life. It is also a very memorable event for every parent. When babies show signs of readiness for solid foods, many moms and dads feel happy and excited. However, some may feel a little worried because not all parents know what kind of food to feed their baby, nor how to prepare it. Old and new parents alike often rely on store-bought baby food and then stick to that until the child is ready to eat regular foods.

Another concern about introducing solid foods to babies is the fact that there is really no definite time to start feeding your baby solids. All babies are unique and will show signs of readiness for food at different times. Sadly, many parents rely on stated dates or ages for introducing solid foods to babies. As a result, they begin feeding their babies solid foods either too early or too late. Somehow it has become a common practice to start feeding babies solid foods at six months, however, babies can exhibit signs of readiness for solid food earlier than that and some babies may not be ready at six months. It is, therefore, advisable for every parent to be watchful for any and every sign that their baby is, in fact, ready for solid foods.

Introducing solid foods to babies in their first year is very important but its role is really not about providing calories, protein, fats, and carbohydrates. Breast milk is still the most important food of babies at this stage and it provides all the nutrients that the child needs. The role of solid foods is more about introducing the young child to new food aromas, textures, and flavors.

Just to clarify, don't let the word "solid" confuse you. Solid food is considered everything beyond what's fed through the baby bottle. Solid baby food is really referring to the blended or mashed baby foods that you often see in those cute little glass baby jars at the grocery store. But better yet, why not make a more fresh, nutritious, and delicious version at home?

For those first-time moms and dads out there, who have no idea what food to prepare for their babies, here is a cookbook that contains recipes of delicious and nutritious baby foods. These are baby food recipes that are low-cost, easy to prepare, and ones that your baby will actually love!

Chapter 1: Baby Food Recipes for Six to Nine Months

Creamy Avocado Fruit Mash

You will need 10 minutes to prepare the ingredients and another 20 minutes to cook. This baby food recipe only takes 30 minutes to make.

Avocados are a rich source of magnesium for healthy bones and it helps in the regulation of blood pressure. It is also a great source of potassium and folate. Serve your baby various avocado recipes and watch your child enjoy avocado's distinctly wonderful taste!

Ingredients:

- 1 pear, peeled, cored and diced
- 1 apple peeled, cored and diced
- 1 whole avocado, peeled and diced
- 1/3 cup of water

How to Prepare:

1. Put the diced pear and into a small pot and add some water.
2. Allow to simmer until the fruits are tender. That takes 10 minutes.
3. Put all the contents of the saucepan into a food processor and make a smooth puree.
4. Place the fruit puree in a bowl and put in the avocado.
5. Mash and serve.

This recipe makes 6 servings.☐

Delicious Cheese, Potato, and Cauliflower Puree

You will need 10 minutes to prepare the ingredients and another 15 minutes to cook. This baby food recipe only takes 25 minutes to make.

Do you have a hungry baby? This puree might just be the best food to prepare. It's a little thicker than the usual vegetable purees and it is certainly very filling and nutritious.

Ingredients:

- 5 tbsp. of milk
- 1 big potato cut in small cubes
- 1 and 1/2 cup of cheddar cheese, shredded
- 1/4 cauliflower head, cut in florets

How to Prepare:

1. Steam the potato cubes for 5 minutes.
2. Put in the cauliflower in the steamer with the potatoes. Spread these evenly and cover. Steam for 10 minutes.
3. Place the steamed vegetables in a blender and put in the cheese as well as the milk. Create a thick puree but add some more milk if needed.
4. Put the puree in individual containers and refrigerate.
5. To serve, just thaw and then reheat. Let it cool before serving.

This baby food recipe makes 6 servings.

Yummy Avocado Soup

You will need 3 minutes to prepare the ingredients and another 5 minutes to cook. This baby food recipe only takes 8 minutes to make.

One of the best fruits that you can give your baby is the avocado. These fruits are wonderful sources of potassium, magnesium, and folate. These help to regulate blood pressure and help strengthen the bones. Moreover, your baby will relish its distinct flavor!

Ingredients:

- 1 cup of vegetable stock, preferably homemade
- 1 ripe avocado, peeled and mashed
- 1/2 cup of milk, breast milk or formula
- a little chopped coriander (cilantro)

How to Prepare:

1. Put the vegetable stock in a small pot and warm.
2. Put in the mashed avocado and then stir.
3. Add the milk and then stir.
4. Sprinkle a little coriander on top.
5. Cool and serve.

This baby food recipe makes 4 servings.

Delightful Chicken Puree

You will need 10 minutes to prepare the ingredients and another 25 minutes to cook. This baby food recipe only takes 35 minutes to make.

This recipe is another delicious way to introduce chicken to your baby. Mix it with some sweet potatoes and you create a yummy meal that your child will love. It's also rich in iron and protein.

Ingredients:

- 2 pieces of chicken thighs
- 2 cups of water or chicken broth
- 1 tbsp. of olive oil
- 1/2 cup of tomato puree
- 1/4 cup of sliced leek
- 1 cup of dried apricots, halved
- 1 and 1/2 cups of chopped sweet potato

How to Prepare:

1. Debone the chicken and remove the skin and fat too.
2. Cut the chicken meat into chunks.
3. In a pan, heat the olive oil and start by sautéing the leeks. Do this for 4 minutes.
4. Put in the chicken and sauté for about 2 minutes. Do this until the chicken meat turns white on all sides.
5. Add in the sweet potato and again, sauté for a minute.
6. Put in the chicken broth, tomato puree, and the apricots. Stir and bring to a boil.
7. Simmer for 15 minutes.
8. Transfer to a blender and make a puree.

This baby food recipe makes 2 and ½ cups.

Yam and Sweet Potato Mash

You will need 10 minutes to prepare the ingredients and another 20 minutes to cook. This baby food recipe only takes 30 minutes to make.

Yams and sweet potatoes are affordable and are always available at the food market. Moreover, these are very easy to cook, and every mom will have no problem making a meal for her baby with these in the kitchen. Yams and sweet potatoes are rich in calcium, magnesium, folate, vitamin A, and selenium. This recipe is great for a very hungry baby!

Ingredients:

- 1 small sweet potato
- 1 small yam
- 1 tbsp. butter
- ¼ cup milk, breast milk or formula

How to Prepare:

1. Clean and peel the sweet potato and yam.
2. Cut the sweet potato and yam in medium sized cubes.
3. Put these in a pot and add some water.
4. Allow this to boil and let simmer until tender. That takes a total of 15 minutes.
5. Remove from pot and place in a bowl.
6. Mash the boiled sweet potato and yam until all big chunks are gone.
7. Add the milk and butter and mash until a smooth consistency is attained.
8. Serve when cooled.
9. Store the remaining mash in a container and keep in a refrigerator. Thaw for the next serving.

This baby food makes 8 servings.☐

Delicious Milk and Brown Rice Cereal

You will need 10 minutes to prepare the ingredients and another 10 minutes to cook. This baby food recipe only takes 20 minutes to make.

Brown rice is good for babies and a brown rice cereal can provide a lot of nutrients for a young child. It is rich in vitamins A, B C, and D. It is also a good source of potassium, iron, calcium, carbohydrate, protein, and magnesium. Here is an easy-to-prepare brown rice recipe for your little one.

Ingredients:

- 1/2 cup organic brown rice
- 1 cup milk, breast milk or formula
- 1 cup of water

How to Prepare:

1. Put the brown rice in a blender and grind it until the rice grains are finely ground. You can also use a spice grinder in lieu of a blender.
2. Boil 1 cup of water and add 4 tbsp. of the finely ground brown rice. Store the rest of the ground brown rice for later use.
3. Stir continuously until it reaches a creamy texture. Make sure that no lumps are formed.
4. Remove from pot, put in a bowl, and add milk according to preference.

This baby food recipe makes 1 serving only. Discard any leftover.

Lip-smacking Superfoods Puree

You will need 10 minutes to prepare the ingredients and another 11 minutes to cook. This baby food recipe only takes 21 minutes to make.

What are superfoods? These are foods that are great sources of antioxidants as well as vitamins and minerals. This recipe is a sure winner because babies love it and parents are happy that their baby is getting all the right nutrients that can be found in a meal.

Ingredients:

- 3/4 cup of ground turkey
- 1 handfuls of washed spinach leaves, not dried
- 1 and 1/2 sweet potato, cut into cubes
- 1 small onion, minced
- 2 tsp. of olive oil

How to Prepare:

1. Steam the sweet potato for 6 minutes. Set aside the water.
2. In a large frying pan, heat the olive oil and add in the onion and turkey. Stir-fry for 3 minutes.
3. Put in the spinach and sauté for another 3 minutes.
4. Add the steamed sweet potato as well as 4 tbsp. of the steaming water. Simmer for 5 minutes.
5. Place all contents in a blender and make a puree. Add more steaming water, if needed.
6. Keep in individual containers and freeze.
7. To serve, heat a portion using a pot or place in the microwave.
8. Check the temperature and serve.

This baby food recipe makes 5 baby portions.

Sweet Carrots Puree

You will need 3 minutes to prepare the ingredients and another 30 minutes to cook. This baby food recipe takes 33 minutes to make.

Carrots are nutritious. It is rich in beta carotene and it is an absolute must in your baby's diet because it will help the eyes stay healthy. Moreover, carrots are delicious and babies as well as toddlers love it. Here is a recipe that you can do for babies 6 months onwards.

Ingredients:

- 1 small piece of carrot, peeled, cut in thick strips
- ¼ cup milk, breast milk or formula

How to Prepare:

1. If you have a vegetable steamer, place the carrots in it and steam for 20 minutes until tender. If you don't have a steamer, you can just boil the carrots using any pot for 20 minutes or until tender.
2. Remove the carrots and set aside the liquid.
3. Place the carrots in a food processor, process, and gradually add the liquid used for its steaming. Add the amount of liquid you need to reach the consistency that you desire. You can also substitute the liquid with breast milk or formula to make it sweeter and more nutritious.
4. Process until a smooth consistency is reached.
5. Serve a portion and store the remaining in a container. Keep refrigerated until baby's next meal.

This baby food recipe makes 2 servings.

Chapter 2: Baby Food Recipes for Ten to Twelve Months

Mouthwatering Banana, Melon, and Mango Puree

You will need 10 minutes to prepare the ingredients and another 3 minutes to do the recipe. This baby food recipe only takes 13 minutes to make.

Mangoes are known for their sweet taste. These yellow tropical fruits are good sources of Vitamins A, B6 and B vitamins, C, magnesium, potassium, and probiotic fiber. Babies love mangoes, however, parents should look out for allergic reactions. Mangoes can be introduced at 6 months, but because of possible allergies, most parents wait until their babies are 10 months old. Here is a delicious mango recipe for your baby to enjoy!

Ingredients:

- 1 slice of melon, peeled and cut in small cubes
- 1 ripe mango, remove seed, cut in cubes
- ¾ ripened, sweet banana, peeled, diced
- A drop of vanilla (optional)

How to Prepare:

1. Place the melon, mango, and banana in a blender.
2. Create a smooth puree.
3. Add vanilla (optional).
4. Serve a portion and store the remaining puree in individual containers.
5. Freeze and thaw at room temperature for the next serving.

This baby food recipe makes 5 servings.

Appetizing Red Lentils with Tomatoes and Carrots

You will need 5 minutes to prepare the ingredients and another 25 minutes to cook. This baby food recipe only takes 30 minutes to make.

Rich sources of antioxidants are carrots and tomatoes. Lycopene, an antioxidant, is found in tomatoes and this is very beneficial for the skin and for the body. Red lentils are sources of iron, fiber, and folate. This recipe is highly nutritious and best for you developing baby.

Ingredients:

- 1 cup of coconut milk
- 1 tbsp. of olive oil
- 1/2 cup of red lentils
- 2 large tomatoes, skinned, seeds removed, and chopped
- ¼ tsp. of ground coriander
- 1 and 1/2 carrots, grated
- 2 cups of water or vegetable broth if available
- ¼ tsp. of ground cumin (optional)

How to Prepare:

1. In a saucepan, heat the oil and sauté the carrots and tomatoes until these are soft. This will often take 5 minutes.
2. Put in the cumin (optional) and the coriander and cook for half a minute.
3. Add in the broth, lentils, and coconut milk. Mix well.
4. Bring to a boil and then simmer for 20 minutes, constantly stirring. Do this until the lentils are soft.
5. Add water when needed.
6. Allow to cool and then place all contents of the pan in a blender. You can also mash it until you reach the desired consistency.
7. The puree is best served warm.

To store, just place in containers and freeze.

To serve, thaw at room temperature for an hour or you can also use a microwave. Reheat and allow to slightly cool before serving.

This baby food recipe makes 4 to 5 baby portions.

Flavorsome Pumpkin and Rice Mash

You will need 20 minutes to prepare the ingredients and another 3 minutes to do the recipe. This baby food recipe takes 23 minutes to make.

Pumpkin is rich in vitamins A, C, and K. Including pumpkin in your diet and will give you and your baby a regular supply of iron, potassium, magnesium, phosphorus, and calcium. Pumpkin has a great flavor and babies adore its creamy texture.

Ingredients:

- 1 small, thin slice of pumpkin, peeled, cubed
- 1 cup of rice, washed
- ¼ cup chicken or vegetable stock

How to Prepare:

1. Cook the rice the regular way. That will take 20 minutes.
2. While the rice is cooking, boil the pumpkin cubes until it becomes tender. That takes 10 minutes.
3. When the rice and the pumpkin are both cooked, get 2 tbsp. of cooked rice and place in a small bowl.
4. Add the pumpkin to it and mash until the rice and the pumpkin are thoroughly mixed.
5. Add the chicken or vegetable stock to the mashed rice and pumpkin to create a smooth texture.
6. Cool and serve.

This baby food recipe makes 1 serving only. Discard any leftover. □

Delectable Poached Salmon

You will need 5 minutes to prepare the ingredients and another 10 minutes to cook. This baby food recipe only takes 15 minutes to make.

Salmon is a good addition to your baby's diet at this stage because it contains omega-3s. In addition, this fish is so easy to cook and flake and is rich in all sorts of vitamins and minerals.

Ingredients:

- 1 piece of salmon
- 2 cups of vegetable broth

How to Prepare:

1. Simmer the vegetable broth.
2. Put in the salmon and cook for 7 minutes. Turn over the fish to make sure all parts are evenly cooked. Simmer for an additional 3 minutes.
3. Place the fish in a plate and remove the skin, bones, and any dark meat.
4. Flake the salmon and serve.

This baby food recipe makes 2 to 3 servings.

Nutritious Green Peas Puree

You will need 1 minute to prepare the ingredients and another 11 minutes to do the recipe. This baby food recipe only takes 12 minutes to make.

Green peas may not be the favorite of babies, but these are certainly the best baby food due to its nutritional value. Peas contain vitamins A, B1, B6, C, and K for stronger bones. With this delicious and nutritious recipe, your baby will begin to enjoy green peas too!

Ingredients:

- 1/2 cup of green peas
- ¼ cup chicken broth or vegetable stock

How to Prepare:

1. Steam the peas using a steamer. You can use a regular pot and just boil the peas in case a steamer is not available. Cover and steam for 6 minutes.
2. Once the peas are cooked and soft, remove from pot or steamer.
3. Create a puree by putting the peas in a food processor. Add in the chicken broth until the desired consistency is attained.
4. Serve a portion and store in a container the remaining puree. Keep refrigerated and just thaw or heat for the next meal.

This baby food recipe makes 4 servings.

Poached Chicken Balls

You will need 25 minutes to prepare the ingredients and another 5 minutes to cook. This baby food recipe only takes 30 minutes to make.

There are numerous first finger foods that you can offer your baby. Meatballs are among the best that you should introduce to your child. However, the usual meatballs style may be too difficult to chew for babies. Therefore, it is best to poach it and make the meatballs more tender and perfect for your young children.

Ingredients:

- 4 cups of chicken broth
- 1 onion, diced
- A dash of pepper
- 1 tsp. of olive oil
- ¼ tsp. of fresh thyme leaves
- 3/4 cup of ground chicken
- 4 tbsp. of grated parmesan cheese
- 1/2 apple, grated
- 3/4 cup of bread crumbs

How to Prepare

1. Sauté the onion for 6 minutes. Set aside in a food processor and allow to cool.
2. Put in the apple, thyme, parmesan, bread crumbs, and chicken. Add pepper according to preference.
3. Process the food until all ingredients are well mixed.
4. Use a teaspoon to create small balls with the mixture.
5. Boil the broth in a pot.
6. Put in the chicken balls and poach for 5 minutes or until cooked.
7. Remove and let it cool. Serve.
8. Store by placing in a container and then refrigerate.
9. To serve, thaw at room temperature for a couple of hours.

This baby food recipe makes 20 meatballs.

Yummy Green Beans and Meat Puree

You will need 1 minute to prepare the ingredients and another 25 minutes to cook. This baby food recipe only takes 26 minutes to make.

Green beans are great sources of Vitamins A, B6, B12, D, calcium, iron, and magnesium. The thing about green beans, though, is that it can be very fibrous and so moms may face a challenge in trying to get it to have a smooth consistency. Nevertheless, here's a recipe that your baby will surely love.

Ingredients:

- 7 pieces of green beans, trimmed
- ¼ cup pork broth
- 1 small piece of pork

How to Prepare:

1. Boil the green beans for 15 minutes or until tender. You can also use a vegetable steamer if you have it.
2. Remove the beans from the pot or steamer but set aside the water used for steaming.
3. From a precooked pork stew, get one small piece of meat and ¼ cup of the broth.
4. Cut the meat in cubes and place in a food processor. Add the green beans and create a smooth puree. Add in the broth until desired consistency of the puree is attained.
5. Serve a portion and place the remaining puree in individual containers for freezing.
6. For the next meals, just heat using a microwave.

This baby recipe makes 3 servings.

Flavorsome Butternut Squash and Brown Rice Mash

You will need 5 minutes to prepare the ingredients and another 20 minutes to cook. This baby food recipe only takes 25 minutes to make.

Among the reasons that moms need to include butternut squash in their baby's diet is that this vegetable is rich in vitamins A, B6, B12, C, and D. It is also a good source of calcium, iron, and magnesium. Butternut squash baby food recipes are easy-to-prepare and that is another reason to try this mouthwatering recipe.

Ingredients:

- 1 whole, small Butternut Squash, peeled and cubed
- 1 cup milk, breast milk or formula
- 1 cup cooked brown rice

How to Prepare:

1. Boil or steam the butternut squash for 15 minutes or until tender. Remove from pot or steamer once tender.
2. Get a cup of cooked brown rice and put it in a bowl. Mash until your reach a sticky consistency.
3. Add the butternut squash in the bowl of rice and continue to mash with a spoon or fork. Put in the milk to create a smooth puree. Add more milk according to your preference.
4. Serve 1 to 2 tbsp. to your baby and keep the rest in individual containers for freezing. For the next servings, just take out the individual containers and reheat contents using a microwave.

This baby food recipe makes 6 to 8 servings.

Tasty Fish and Rice Mash

You will need 1 minute to prepare the ingredients and another 20 minutes to cook. This baby food recipe only takes 21 minutes to make.

Fish is rich in niacin, phosphorus, vitamin B12, selenium, and protein. Moms should introduce meat and fish to babies as young as 6 months because of the nutritional benefits as well as the new taste and texture that babies will love. Here is a tried-and-tested recipe for babies who are ready for a new flavor.

Ingredients:

- ½ cup Tilapia fish meat (you can use other kinds of fish)
- ¼ cup cooked rice

How to Prepare:

1. Put the fish in a pot and steam or broil for 15 minutes.
2. Debone the fish and make sure that the meat is free from any small fish bones.
3. Put the cooked rice in a bowl and mash. Add in the Tilapia meat and continue to mash.
4. Add some vegetable stock or water to create a smooth consistency. Add more stock according to taste and preference.
5. Serve.

This baby food makes 1 serving only. Discard any leftover.

Finally, I'd like to thank you for reading this book! If you enjoyed it or found it helpful, I'd greatly appreciate it if you'd take a moment to leave a review on Amazon. Thank you!

Made in the USA
Las Vegas, NV
12 December 2021

37410237R00028